# Leapfrogging the COMPETITION

## 9 Proven Ways to Unleash Change and Innovation

**Mac Anderson | John J. Murphy**

simple truths
small books. BIG IMPACT.

Photo Credits
Internals: pages 2–3, Rawpixel/Shutterstock; page 11, Sfio Cracho/Shutterstock; page 18, Pressmaster/Shutterstock; page 59, g-stockstudio/Shutterstock; page 67, YanLev/Shutterstock; page 92, Rawpixel/Shutterstock; pages 102–103, Iakov Kalinin/Shutterstock.

Published by Simple Truths, an imprint of Sourcebooks, Inc.
P.O. Box 4410, Naperville, Illinois 60567-4410
(630) 961-3900
Fax: (630) 961-2168
www.sourcebooks.com

Printed and bound in China.
QL 10 9 8 7 6 5 4 3 2 1

"The beginning of success is realizing that the way it is now is not the way it has to be."

—*Napoleon Hill*

# Contents

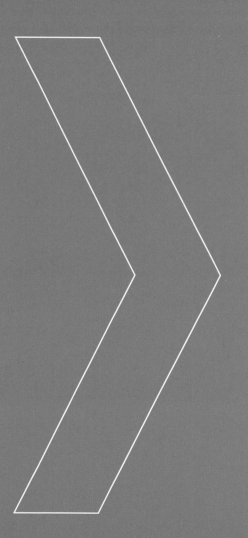

"Only those who will
risk going too far can
possibly find out how
far one can go."

—T. S. Eliot

# Introduction:
# Leapfrogging the Competition

Winning in the long run requires more than talent, money, and resources—especially when the competition gets really tough and the playing field is continuously changing. Yesterday's best practices might be obsolete today, not unlike a fax machine or a floppy disk.

The upside to all of this change is fascinating—for the entrepreneur and innovator. The sweet smell of opportunity and success is captivating. However, it might be terrifying for the play-it-safe manager or middleman.

The purpose of this book is to help answer the questions **Why do some companies succeed greatly while others in the same field stagnate?** and, more importantly, **What can we do about it now to reduce risk and avoid failure?** These are not always simple questions to answer; however, there are common denominators that will help to answer the "why" behind **leapfrogging the competition.**

I've been an entrepreneur for the last forty years. I've been fortunate to have launched three different start-ups, each becoming a leader in its niche. As you might imagine, there were a lot of peaks and valleys along the way and even a near-death experience.

To help me explore the answers to the common denominators behind leapfrogging the competition, I recruited John Murphy, one of my favorite business authors. While I have enjoyed the real-life experience of being in the trenches as an entrepreneur, John has spent his adult life coaching hundreds of well-known companies on how to become all they can be through his firm Venture Management Consultants. He's seen it all—the good, the bad, and the ugly. Combining our collective experiences and drawing from the wisdom of others will help us to uncover the "whys" behind those who succeed and the companies that fade into oblivion.

We all know the world is changing at a rapid pace. What are the things you can do to get the edge on your competition to ensure long-term success? This book is not about everything you need to know but what John and I feel are **the most important things.**

Remember, leapfrogging the competition isn't just about outsmarting the external forces against you and your business: it is also about leapfrogging your own resistance to change. Sometimes it's best to make the change, not manage it.

Take the leap. Get out in front. The view is terrific, and there's a lot less traffic.

All the best,

Mac Anderson

Founder, Simple Truths and Successories

# 1

"Any intelligent fool can make things bigger and more complex. It takes a touch of genius—and a lot of courage—to move in the opposite direction."

—*Albert Einstein*

# Know Your Market and Customer

Rule number one in any successful business is to know who is paying you and precisely what they are paying you for. Without a crystal clear understanding of *value in the eyes of the customer*, non-value-added activity and waste will inevitably creep into every process, practice, and function in the business. Intelligent, motivated, and well-intentioned people will come up with ideas and procedures to make their work easier and more efficient without linking it to the bigger picture—the end user! They will add steps, meetings, reports, tools, metrics, and complexity to the business without ever really considering who wants to pay for it.

To leapfrog the competition and truly *wow* the people paying you for your efforts, it is absolutely essential to understand how everything you do fits into the bigger picture. Isolated, independent activity, even with the most positive intentions and logic, can silently and subtly rob us blind. It is, in many cases, our greatest form of competition—our own creation of wasted time and activity. It is like Walt Kelly wrote in *Pogo*: "We have met the enemy, and he is us."

Smart business leaders also learn to understand the mystery and power of *paradox* hidden within many global best practices. It is uncovering this mystery of paradox that allows astute business leaders to "get it" when so many others do not.

# HERE ARE SOME EXAMPLES OF THE MYSTERY OF PARADOX:

1. We know how to work less and accomplish more.

2. We know how to go slower and move faster.

3. We know how to sell more with fewer salespeople and efforts.

4. We know how to get customers to chase us!

5. We know how to communicate more effectively, often without saying a word.

Mysteries such as these help us to leverage our talent, prioritize our efforts, and manage our time in optimal ways.

Of course, the referee in all of this is the market—the ultimate playing field.

To be truly successful, we need to know what the market wants, needs, and values—sometimes before the market has even figured this out. Great innovators recognize that the customer is *not* always right, another paradox. Henry Ford once said that if he had asked his customers what they wanted, they would have said a faster horse. Steve Jobs never would have offered us an iPod or an iPad if he had waited for customers to ask for one. Instead, these clever business leaders uncovered latent market needs and customer desires before anyone asked. There is no more powerful way to leapfrog your competition than to offer something of value to the market that no one else has yet provided. Getting there first is the name of the game among great innovators and transformational leaders. Just ask companies like Blockbuster, Borders Books, Circuit City, Kodak, Smith-Corona, and hundreds more. The only problem is that there is no one left to ask; these companies were outsmarted.

Clever entrepreneurs and business leaders recognize that smart businesses work backward to some extent—another counterintuitive paradigm shift that many people find confusing. A shift in perception or application (like an entirely new business model or transformational technology) can set all competitors back to zero. Just look at what companies like Amazon, Google, Uber, Tesla, Square, PayPal, Pandora, YouTube, and so many others are doing to the competition. These disruptive companies are transforming the world by challenging the underlying assumptions driving many

business models and setting new expectations. In addition to the common practice of focusing inwardly on departmental efficiencies and productivities, they are starting with the end in mind and linking everything they do to the ultimate goal in any business: creating customer advocates and promoters in the market. When your customers start selling your brand for you through positive word of mouth, you are well on your way to significant growth and prosperity. You walk the walk and let others talk the talk.

In a recent kaizen event, John encouraged his client to include an actual customer in the event. In past improvement efforts, this client had not considered this option. Instead, they were using common tools like Net Promoter Score (NPS) surveys, customer complaints, and other lagging indicators to evaluate performance. So this was a shift in thinking and a very different approach. Another shift in thinking was to invite a detractor rather than someone who would recommend no change.

The invited customer was very unhappy and gladly revealed why she was a detractor. She showed the team her supplier auditing process and the three critical metrics she used to evaluate performance. The team quickly realized that their company was failing in all three areas. This was takeaway number one. Takeaway number two was that of the thirty-three internal metrics the company was using to evaluate their performance, not one of the customer's three metrics were included. Wow! This was an enlightening moment of truth for the team, which immediately led to several rapid changes aligning expectations, priorities, and practices with the expectations of the customer—a company with 80,000 employees and significant revenue. This customer also was getting ready to say good-bye to the client.

Six weeks later, the client was scoring high on all three indicators, and the customer had shifted from a detractor to a promoter. She also attended the next two kaizen events to help take performance to an even higher level.

 Knowing your market and your customers is critical to growing your business and outsmarting your competition.

## Be wise.

## Beware.

## Start with the END in mind!

# CHECKLIST FOR SUCCESS

✓ Know what the market needs, and have the research to back it up.

✓ Understand your customers as well as, if not better than, they know themselves.

✓ Know your customers' customers.

✓ Research your customers' problems, needs, and concerns.

✓ Invite your customers to participate in product and process improvements.

✓ Find ways to know immediately if there is a problem with a customer, and act quickly to resolve it at the root cause level.

✓ Align your value proposition with what the market and customers want and are willing to pay for. There is no doubt about who is paying your company and exactly what they are paying you for. This gives your company clarity of vision, focus, prioritization, and alignment.

# 2 〉

"Hard work and best efforts without guidance of profound knowledge may well be the root of our ruination. There is no substitute for knowledge."

—W. Edwards Deming

# Know Your Competition and Limitations

Competition can take many forms. It can appear as an *external* force against you—from another company competing with you for market share or a new technology offered by another source. It can appear as an *internal* force against you—fear, doubt, disbelief, ignorance, waste, non-value-added activity, and inefficiency. Competition can even appear in the form of another company that has nothing to do with your industry. Like it or not, your customers compare you to everyone else they do business with. Consciously and subconsciously, they wonder why you can't be Disney friendly, Subway flexible, or FedEx fast. If I can click on a link to see where my Domino's pizza or my UPS package is, why can't I click on a link to know where the shipment from your company is? If I have a smartphone, why can't I have a smart garage or a smart stove? If I can pay bills, check into a hotel, board a plane, and buy groceries with a card, why can't I do the same thing with my fingerprint? Questions like these reveal who and what our real competition is. It is any force against us, anything holding us back from really wowing our customers and setting others back to zero.

The word *empowerment* might be one of the most overused words in business jargon today. Yet, despite its popularity, many struggle to understand what it is really about. Empowerment is not about adding more power, authority, and responsibility to people. It is about subtracting the forces against us—removing obstacles and eliminating the barriers to success. The essence of empowerment is killing obsolete and ineffective policies, meetings, limitations, and reports while engaging people on the front line in authentic kaizen events where real change is made before the event ends. It is about going far beyond outdated, reactive suggestion boxes and open-door policies to proactive blitzes on waste and inefficient value streams.

## TRUE EMPOWERMENT

is about helping people realize that they have abundant power and ingenuity within and around them. The key is to get out of your own way and let energy and empowerment flow!

Over the years, many psychological studies have suggested that the average human being achieves only 10 to 18 percent of his or her true potential in life. Stop and contemplate this. Talk about a significant amount of waste. Where is the remaining talent and potential going? And why?

Great companies and business leaders are very clear on the various forms of competition. As a result, they are crystal clear on finding ways to attack and eliminate it. Take the Disney organization, for example. Disney's mission is to make people happy. When Disney accomplishes this, their customers become advocates and promoters. This means that not only do they tend to return to Disney, providing more revenue and growth, but they also advocate Disney to friends and family. They sell Disney, providing even more revenue and growth!

So how does an organization like Disney do this? How do they continue to leapfrog the competition? They pay attention to the forces against them. They pay attention to the moments of truth, or magic moments, as they like to call them. This translates into "anything and everything that makes people *unhappy*," since the organization's mission is to make people happy. This is a very different way to think about competition. Yet, it is no different from how many world-class athletes, performers, and professionals see it. True competition is often right in front of us and within us, and yet we fail to see it. At Disney, this translates into things like litter, long lines, lost cars in the parking lots, lost children in the parks, sunburns, boredom, and rude service—specific things that are within our control. As a result, Disney has preprogrammed responses for people who forget where they parked or if they get separated from a child. Disney is renowned for being clean because of its efficient maintenance practices, and rarely do people have to stand in the direct sunlight while being entertained in line.

## Stop and ask yourself:

What is your mission as a business, and what is in your way?

While paying attention to the ever-changing market and external competition is critical, do you tend to the forces against you in an immediate way?

What is obstructing flow in your business in the following areas—product, service, information, cash, and even people?

What is holding you back?

What are your limitations, including any limiting beliefs?

> **What** assumptions **are you making that drive policy, procedure, design, measurement, marketing, compensation, hiring, training, incentive, capability, and competition?**

And entrepreneurs, managers, and business owners—beware! Often, it is you who are holding the organization back without even knowing it!

# CHECKLIST FOR SUCCESS

✓ Continuously look for and uncover the forces against your business.

✓ Understand that competition is both external and internal.

✓ Recognize that customers may be comparing you to other providers that have nothing to do with your industry.

✓ Realize that empowerment is more about removing obstacles than adding authority and complexity.

✓ Continuously find ways to remove obstacles, barriers, and constraints.

✓ Benchmark best practices inside and outside your industry. Always look for ideas on how to improve what you do and innovate new advancements.

✓ Exercise intuition and imagination to connect the dots between seemingly unrelated best practices in other industries and your own business. Be on the lookout for new, creative applications that others have not yet uncovered.

✓ Understand the critical importance of flow, and find ways to accelerate it.

# 3

"Making the simple complicated is commonplace; making the complicated simple, awesomely simple, that's creativity."

—*Charles Mingus*

# Simplify Your Mission

Companies that leapfrog their competition know the value of simplicity. In fact, those companies that set the pace for their competitors know firsthand that less is almost always more. Take consultants Joe Calhoon and Bruce Jeffrey, for instance. They have built their business around the importance of simplicity, specializing in creating a simple one-page strategic plan for their clients. Here are six key elements they include in their simplified plans:

**Vision:** A clear picture of your destination

**Mission:** The driving purpose of your business

**Values:** The guide you use for decision-making and how you treat one another

**Objectives:** The numbers you track

**Strategies:** The paths you've decided to take

**Priorities:** The work that needs to get done and who needs to do it

According to Calhoon and Jeffrey, they've never seen a business plan that was too short, but they have seen hundreds that would make an acceptable cure for insomnia. They also said that they have never encountered a company that couldn't fit their plan on one page once the management team understood the process. Does it take a little more time to drill down? Sure it does, but it's well worth it, because it forces you to cut out a lot of verbiage and make decisions on what's important.

A simplified strategic plan crystallizes the company's vision for your employees, helping to create the momentum that can make your company's goals a reality. The late Roberto Goizueta, CEO and president of the Coca-Cola Company for seventeen years, was a master of encapsulating complex ideas and presenting them in concise, compelling language. In doing so, he generated more wealth for shareholders than any CEO in the company's history—all while making Cola-Cola one of the most prominent trademarks in the world.

Roberto was best known for his oft-repeated description of Coke's infinite growth potential:

Each of the world's six billion *(now seven billion)* people drink on average sixty-four ounces of fluids daily, of which only two ounces are Coca-Cola.

LEAPFROGGING THE COMPETITION

Coke's employees were blown away by the originality and audacity of the statement when Goizueta first spoke it. Eventually, closing the sixty-two-ounce gap became a centerpiece of inspiration and motivation within the company.

Simplicity of mission and vision applies, no matter what business you are in. Nordstrom, the department store known for their great service, is another example of a company that has mastered the art of simplifying for success. When it comes to taking care of the customer, Nordstrom has only one rule for employees: use good judgment in all situations. One Nordstrom employee summed it up: "Because we don't have many rules, we don't have to worry about breaking them. We are judged on our performance, not our obedience to orders."

In every area of our lives, simplicity just makes life simpler. But, in business, simplicity in your mission can translate to success. It ensures that your team actually understands your business direction. That knowledge, coupled with action, is what will set your business apart from your competitors.

# SIM·PLI·FY

# CHECKLIST FOR SUCCESS

✓ Strive to create a one-page strategic plan.

✓ Skip the rhetoric and drill down to the metrics that really set your business apart.

✓ Take the time to communicate your vision and mission to your employees so that everyone is working on the same page.

✓ Free employees up from extraneous rules so they can translate that simplicity to their interactions with customers.

✓ Get down to basics. In the end, the flawless execution of your organization's basic tenets will differentiate your business.

# 4

"Good leaders must first become good servants."

—Robert K. Greenleaf

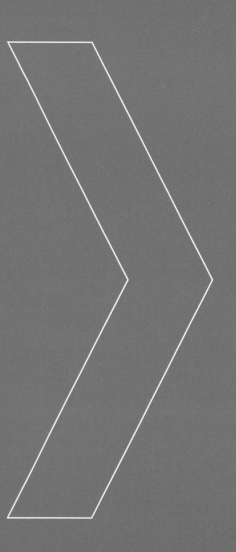

# Think Serve, Not Lead

When your employees observe you as a leader, who do they see? Someone focused only on going up the organizational ladder? Or a servant leader, someone committed to serving both your customers and your employees?

That's the philosophy of Cheryl Bachelder, the CEO of Popeyes Louisiana Kitchen, which has more than 2,000 franchises worldwide. She credits being a servant leader with helping her turn around the struggling restaurant chain—improving the profitability of Popeyes restaurants

40 percent in terms of real dollars. In her book *Dare to Serve: How to Drive Superior Results by Serving Others*, Bachelder recounts a conversation with one of her mentors about the importance of creating a service culture:

> He said to me, "Cheryl, have you considered your influence? Take the number of employees who work for Popeyes and multiply that by the number of hours in a workweek—and then by the number of weeks in a year.
>
> "You have more influence than you know. Are you using that influence for good?
>
> "Think about the math: If you have five full-time people looking to you for leadership, in the year ahead, you have 10,000 hours of influence. You will likely spend more time with these five people than their parents, spouse, teacher, neighbors, or kids.

"If you have fifty full-time people looking to you for leadership, in the year ahead, you have 100,000 hours of influence.

"If you have five hundred full-time people looking to you for leadership, in the year ahead, you have 1,000,000 hours of influence."

My friend is so right. Every leader has exponential opportunities for influence.

Servant leaders use that influence to create effective change by shifting their focus from their own needs to supporting those of their employees. Servant leaders are those others *want* to follow.

In his book *The Right to Lead*, John C. Maxwell points out that an effective leader is someone others can trust to take them where they want to go.

Here are his guidelines for becoming that type of leader:

> **Let go of your ego.** The truly great leaders are not in leadership for personal gain. They lead in order to serve other people.

> **Become a good follower first.** Rare is the effective leader who didn't learn to become a good follower first. That is why a leadership institution such as the United States Military Academy teaches its officers to become effective followers first—and why West Point has produced more leaders than the Harvard Business School.

> **Build positive relationships.** Leadership is influence—nothing more, nothing less. Today's generation of leaders seem particularly aware of this

because title and position mean so little to them. They know intuitively that people go along with people they get along with.

> **Work with excellence.** No one respects and follows mediocrity. Leaders who earn the right to lead give their all to what they do. They bring into play not only their skills and talents, but also great passion and hard work. They perform at the highest level of which they are capable.

> **Rely on discipline, not emotion.** Leadership is often easy during the good times. It's when everything seems to be against you—when you're out of energy and you don't want to lead—that you earn your place as a leader.

> **Make added value your goal.** When you look at the leaders whose names are revered long after they have finished leading, you find that they were men and women who helped people to live better lives and reach their potential. That is the highest calling of leadership— and its highest value.

> **Give your power away.** One of the ironies of leadership is that you become a better leader by sharing whatever power you have, not by saving it all for yourself. If you use your power to empower others, your leadership will extend far beyond your group.

# CHECKLIST FOR SUCCESS

✓ Think serve, not lead.

✓ Make being a servant leader a tenant of your culture, for you and all of your direct reports.

✓ Walk the talk. Let employees see that you put your philosophy in action every day.

✓ Make listening to your employees a priority. You'll discover issues—and solutions—that may not have surfaced otherwise.

✓ Remind yourself daily of the amount of influence you have. Use that influence to create a service culture you and your employees will be proud to be a part of.

# 5

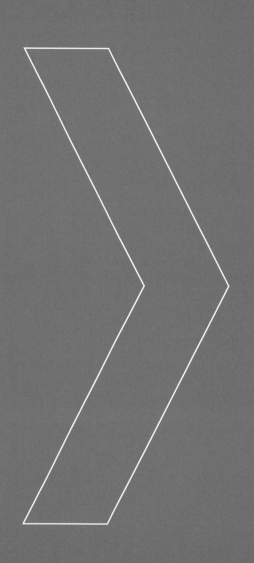

"Time spent on hiring
is time well spent."

—*Robert Half*

# Your Customers Must Come Second— Make Every Hire Count

It's like the chicken-or-the-egg question: Who comes first if you want to achieve business success—your customers or your employees? Herb Kelleher, an industry leader in customer service and one of the founders and former CEO of Southwest Airlines, sheds some light on the answer:

"I always felt that our people came first. Some of the business schools regarded that as a conundrum. They would say, 'Which comes first: your people, your customers, or your shareholders?' And I would say, 'It's not a conundrum. Your people come first, and if you treat them right, they'll treat the customers right, and the customers will come back, and that'll make the shareholders happy.'"

# So what's the first step to putting your employees first?

## Hire the best people—and treat them right!

Howard Schultz, chairman and CEO for Starbucks, understood that the key to the success of his then-fledgling coffee business was to recruit well-educated people who were eager to communicate their passion for coffee. This, he felt, would be his competitive advantage in an industry where turnover was 300 percent a year. To hire the best people, he also knew he must be willing to pay them more than the going wage and offer health benefits that weren't available elsewhere. He saw that part-time people made up two-thirds of his employee base, and no one in the restaurant industry offered benefits to part-timers. Schultz went to work in an effort to sell his board of directors on increasing expenses while most restaurant executives in the 1980s were looking for ways to cut costs. Initially, Starbucks was still losing money. But Schultz was persistent. He was looking long-term and was committed to growing the business with passionate people. He won, and he said many times afterward that this decision was one of the most important decisions, if not *the* most important, that he had made at Starbucks. His employee retention rate was about five times the industry average, but more importantly, he could attract people with great attitudes who made their customers feel welcome and at home.

In his landmark study of companies that made the leap in his book *Good to Great*, author Jim Collins found that great companies focused first on their people:

"We expected that good-to-great leaders would begin by setting a new vision and strategy. We found instead that they **first** got the right people on the bus, the wrong people off the bus, and the right people in the right seats— and **then** they figured out where to drive it. The old adage 'People are your most important asset' turns out to be wrong. People are **not** your most important asset. The **right** people are."

## So how do you get the right people on the bus?

In a 2014 article for the American Management Association, Brian Tracy, one of the top business speakers and authors in the world today, shared the SWAN formula for hiring:

# The **SWAN** Formula

The SWAN formula was recommended some years ago by an executive recruiter named John Swan. It is a good acronym that you can use to improve your selection process.

**S** stands for **SMART**. Hire smart people. How do you tell the intelligence of a candidate? The answer is simple: questions! Intelligent people tend to be more curious than average people.

**W** stands for **WORK HARD**. Look for people who are willing to work hard and who have backgrounds that indicate that they have worked long, hard hours—including evenings and weekends—at previous jobs.

**A** stands for **AMBITION**. The proper candidate is someone who wants to move ahead in life. Ambitious people are willing and eager to take additional training; they are already reading and studying and seeking opportunities to grow, both personally and professionally.

**N** stands for people who are **NICE**. The likability of the candidate is a critical factor and is especially important for people who have to deal with the public or with customers.

In the final analysis, your ability to pick the right people for your team is the key to motivation. You cannot hire the wrong people and then expect to motivate them to be excellent performers for your team. It is much better that you proceed carefully and painstakingly and hire the right people in the first place.

Constantly remind yourself that hiring the right person for your team is your most important job as a manager. With each hire, your credibility and your team's success are on the line.

When hiring someone, start with the premise that attitudes are contagious.

## Then ask yourself one question:

*Is theirs worth catching?*

# CHECKLIST FOR SUCCESS

✓ Remember that your people come first; your customers come second.

✓ The *right* people are your most important asset.

✓ Use the SWAN formula for hiring.

✓ Hiring the right person for your team is your most important job as a manager.

✓ Remember that attitudes are contagious: Is your new hire's attitude worth catching?

"We are what we repeatedly do. Excellence, then, is not an act but a habit."

—*Aristotle*

# Strive for Excellence—Always!

Inherent in any great business is a passion and ongoing desire to do great work. It doesn't matter what business you are in or how long you have been around. There is no substitute for heartfelt commitment and an intelligent business strategy to deliver excellent results. Of course, this is easier said than done. Many people in society today have been conditioned with a just-get-by attitude or B mentality. How does a business leader build excellence into a corporate culture so that it becomes habit and not just an occasional act of heroism?

Start by paying attention to companies doing it really well and consistently. How do top quality hotels hire room attendants, sometimes from very challenging upbringings, and inspire them to clean rooms so carefully and diligently? How do certain valet parking service companies get employees to be so conscientious with other people's cars? How do some retailers and fast-food organizations get minimum-wage employees to treat customers with such respect and courtesy? The answer may seem simple to understand but often reflects another paradox. In order to be flexible (with customers and market demands), we must be rigid and rigorous. Great companies do not fly by the seat of their pants. FedEx cannot pick up a package in Boston and have it delivered on time to a remote destination in San Diego without a highly disciplined business model, system, and structure. Disney cannot effectively accommodate millions of guests from dozens of countries every year without rigorous business practices and carefully orchestrated activities. Walmart cannot pass savings on to consumers, a key component of its relatively simple mission, with sloppy supply-chain management and poor vendor control. To provide excellence in any form, we have to be highly disciplined, discerning, and vigilant.

It takes time, attention, research, awareness, and ongoing discipline to leapfrog your competition by building excellence into your culture. It all starts with knowing your market and ever-changing customer expectations and making this clear to everyone who works in the business. We cannot provide excellence in the eyes of our customers if we are not all clear on who the real customers are and what they really want—especially when market expectations are continually changing. No one today wants an excellent floppy disk made better by the process improvement tools of Six Sigma.

Great companies also know how to simplify their mission so that everyone understands it and uses it to create a timely service culture. This is critical to developing a clearly focused, highly disciplined, lean culture where distractions, waste, and variation are seen as a form of competition. *Time* now becomes a key element in everything we do. Customers value time, so we must too. In addition to wanting reliable quality, excellent service, and competitive pricing, customers tend to want things faster and precisely on time. Thus, LeanSigma has become one of the dominant best practices worldwide. Using our time more wisely can be one of the most significant competitive advantages we have.

# Put another way, we all have twenty-four hours in a day.

The real question becomes how are we using it? Are we using time like an orchestra, to build harmony and balance into our service equation? Are we using time like a championship sports team to execute various initiatives (plays) diligently? Are we finding ways to get more done in less time without tapping out our people? Are we truly working smarter? Or are we using time like many people use closets: Are we filling it with a lot of clutter and outdated things and then wishing we had more space?

A clear mission coupled with meaningful guiding principles and vigilant accountability will cultivate excellence into habit. People just have to know what excellence looks like in terms of specific behaviors—and why it is important. We need context as well as content. We also have to know that it is not optional. It is a core value of the company, and anyone and everyone working in the business will be held accountable for meeting the standards set. Excellence must be very clearly defined and designed into standard work routines and procedures. It cannot be left up to individual interpretation and choice. This is all part of the rigor and discipline of high-performing work cultures. We find and develop best practices, and then everyone follows them until we come up with something better.

We have all experienced the opposite of excellence—lousy service, poor product design, product failure, recurring mistakes, and complex processes that add little, if any, value. Often, it is an individual employee who is then ridiculed or blamed for these undesirable effects. Wise business leaders look deeper than this. We recognize that most people simply operate within whatever system we give them. They follow the policies and procedures. They do the best they can with what they have. But, if an employee is trapped in a poorly designed system or is required to use ineffective tooling, changing people will never solve the real problems. Solving problems inside the box when the box itself (the paradigm, business model, or overall business system) is the problem can be a complete waste of time. To build a culture of excellence, we must design it into everything we do, from strategy to policy to procedure to measurement and reward. A truly good product or service design will *poka-yoke* (Japanese for "mistake-proof") common human errors so that things *cannot* go wrong.

Excellence, then, takes more than an attitude or independent acts of heroism; it requires designing it into your culture for flawless execution.

 Try competing with that!

# CHECKLIST FOR SUCCESS

✓ Benchmark other companies with consistent, global best practices.

✓ Recognize that to create and sustain a culture of excellence, you must *design* it into your business systems, structure, metrics, and operating policies.

✓ Realize that excellence is a moving target. Market needs and expectations are changing. No one today wants a Six Sigma floppy disk.

✓ Know that excellence requires rigor, discipline, and clear accountability.

✓ Time-based management must be incorporated into your business strategy to achieve true excellence.

✓ Do not use time as an excuse to delay high-priority items or rationalize marginal performance.

✓ Recognize that most people work within whatever system they are given. Therefore, if you want to "change the way we do things around here" (culture), you must "change the way we do things around here" (business systems and structure).

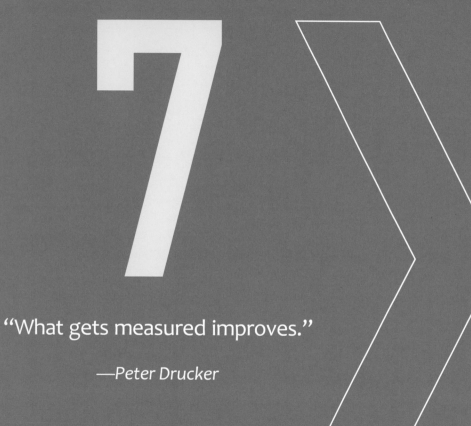

# 7

"What gets measured improves."

—Peter Drucker

# Measure Results and Hold People Accountable

Keeping score is no doubt one of the most critical components to running any successful business. The real question then is what to keep score of. We tend to get what we *inspect*, not what we *expect*. Therefore, we must pay close attention to what we pay attention to!

As cited in an earlier example with one of John's clients, it is essential to pay attention to what your customers are paying attention to. What are they measuring? What is essential to them?

< LEAPFROGGING THE COMPETITION >

> ## How have they specified value?

## Value = f(Q,S,P,T,I)

In most cases, value is a combination of several key factors. Let's call these "buckets." One of these buckets is usually categorized as *quality*, and within the quality bucket, we have variables like consistency, accuracy, reliability, repeatability, predictability, safety, precision, and efficacy. Stop and ask yourself: What are the key variables in the quality bucket in your organization? What really matters to your customers in this category? Recognize that customers will put more weight on one factor over another and one bucket over another. Not all customers are the same. One consumer may choose to buy lunch at McDonald's because he values product consistency, predictable taste, and repeatability, while another consumer may choose a competitor because she has a very different perception of quality.

A second bucket in the value equation is *service*. Like quality, it too has different variables within it. Service can mean an assortment of different things to different people, including order accuracy, friendliness, responsiveness, assurance, empathy, ease of use, first-time resolution of problems, cleanliness, options, and convenience. Some might want a self-service option while others want an 800 number to call. Within each of these buckets is what great companies often call critical to customer (CTC) or critical to measure (CTM) factors. These critical factors must be identified as part of the value proposition and then carefully measured to ensure performance. After all, these factors are typically what your customers are measuring—whether you are or not!

The third bucket is *price*. Customers do pay attention to price, and in many industries, they have become accustomed to getting more for less. The laptop, calculator, or cell phone you buy today typically comes with more features, more battery life, more memory, faster speeds, and lower pricing than it did five or ten years ago. How can this be? It is simply another example of paradox. Wouldn't more features and more capability cost more?

Not when it comes to working smarter! Consider downloading an electronic book or digital movie onto a lightweight tablet. You are often paying less, getting the book faster and accurately, in a much more user-friendly way—all without leaving your seat!

These innovations exist today simply because bold, imaginative, transformational leaders are willing to challenge the status quo and think outside the box. Take the time to examine your pricing strategies. Are you in the paradigm of year-after-year price increases, using cost increases as your rationale? Are you challenging this paradigm and exploring alternatives? Keep in mind, your customers may be asking the same thing or may be under the same pressure.

The next bucket is *time*. Many years ago, time was considered a factor in the service bucket. But with the global acceptance of Lean as a best practice in the 1990s, time has now earned its own spot in the starting lineup. In this bucket, we find factors and CTMs like cycle time, lead time, on-time delivery, inventory turns (how much inventory is sold over a period of time), value-added time as a percentage of total time, hold time, response time, and resolution time. In fact, customers are now putting more and more emphasis on time as a deciding factor in choosing suppliers. Not only do we want it right the first time, easy to service, and priced competitively, but we also want it faster than ever before! Many leading-edge companies today are using time as a critical differentiator in leapfrogging the competition. If Walmart and Target can sell products and get paid for them before the bill on what they just sold is due, that's tough to compete with.

The last bucket is *innovation*. Indeed, innovation was hardly considered a bucket of its own until recently. With the rapid advancement of innovations like the Internet, GPS, wireless technology, gamma-ray scanning, and digital media, who can argue that this isn't one of the most significant ways to leapfrog the competition? Again, just consider some of the great companies who have been left behind. Within the innovation bucket, we find factors like product design and features, intuitive processing (like a smartphone), *poka-yoke*, ease of use, process design, and new value propositions that no one has yet heard of.

**If you really want to WOW your customers and leapfrog the competition, DO NOT MISS THE INNOVATION BUCKET!**

Measuring results must be targeted, prioritized, and clearly impactful on the business in general. Micromanagement does not get you there if you are missing the big picture. Each of these buckets offers clues on what to look for and measure as it relates to the market, your customers, and the cash you generate. Often times when it comes to measuring, less is more.

Top companies use balanced scorecards and relatively simple dashboards to define, monitor, and report key indicators of performance. Are you doing this? What are your top-ten metrics or key performance

indicators? How do you know your business is healthy and in balance? Are you aligned with your customers? Are you using these measures to gain knowledge about your business and adjust as needed? Are these dashboards visible to all on a daily basis? How do people know each and every day that they are on target in terms of what really matters—without having to ask anyone or attend meetings? Is your scoreboard visible, timely, and meaningful to the players on the field? And are you holding yourself and your team accountable for hitting your targets?

# CHECKLIST FOR SUCCESS

✓ Measure what your customers are measuring you on so you are aligned.

✓ Understand that value means different things to different people. Be diligent in determining specifically what value means in the eyes of your customers.

✓ Identify key performance indicators for your business and develop an easy-to-understand dashboard so your team can see how you are doing on a daily basis.

✓ Realize that what gets measured gets managed and what gets managed gets done.

✓ Use measurement to collect meaningful data, gain knowledge about your business, and identify opportunities for ongoing improvement and innovation.

✓ Be more than 95 percent confident of what your business is capable of, based on data.

✓ Use global best practice tools like Statistical Process Control (SPC) and Lean Daily Management (LDM) to help align, monitor, and report performance on a real-time basis.

✓ Hold yourself and your team accountable for hitting clearly defined targets.

"Goals are for the future; values are for now. Goals are set; values are lived. Goals change; values are rocks that you can count on."

—*Sheldon Bowles*

# Reinforce Core Values

Identifying the core values that define your company is one of the most important functions of leadership. They can make or break your long-term success. Core values serve as critical guides for making decisions, and when in doubt, they cut through the fog like a beacon in the night. But, you should also know that gaps between your values and your actions can do more harm than good. In other words, if you talk about building a customer-first culture but fail to do so, you'll lose the respect of your employees and your customers.

Therefore, as a leader, you must select your core values carefully, because once you commit, your credibility is on the line. Here's a real-life example from Mac's years at Successories:

Early on, our motto was: *Quality is the mother…and we don't mess with Mom.* We made a decision, as a company, that our graphics, our paper stock, our color separations, our frames, even our shipping cartons would be of the highest quality.

It was one of our core values.

In 1988, we were at about five million dollars in sales. Cash was tight, and we were watching every penny. Mike McKee, my creative partner and friend, walked into my office with a big smile, holding up a new Successories print that had just come off the press. As we were congratulating each other, my assistant walked in and pointed to an apostrophe in the quote at the bottom of the print. It should have come before the *S* instead of behind it.

To reprint it would have cost five thousand dollars, which we didn't have at the time.

Although we both knew that 999 people out of 1,000 wouldn't notice the misplaced apostrophe, our commitment to quality left us with only one choice—destroy the prints and start over. It was a gut-wrenching decision, given our financial situation, but the right one. It left no doubt with our team that we were willing to walk the talk when it came to quality.

As John G. Blumberg says in *Good to the Core*:

"We go to work each day in organizations with undefined values and wonder why the environment lacks meaningful momentum. We are simply out at sea drifting from one distraction to another. Core values create boundaries. Boundaries create focus, and focus minimizes drift."

Putting your core values into action, especially when the decision is a tough one, is what will help differentiate your company from its competitors. As a leader, that decision falls to you…and your employees *will* notice if your values are just hollow words or true guideposts for all to follow.

Albert Schweitzer was once asked if he thought that leading by example was the main thing in influencing others. He thought for a second and said, "No, it's not the *main* thing… It is the *only* thing."

# CHECKLIST FOR SUCCESS

✓ Determine which behaviors will drive your values forward, and communicate those to all your employees.

✓ Make your core values the guideposts that shape your decisions.

✓ Take every opportunity to reinforce your core values every day.

✓ Lead by example, especially when the going gets tough.

# 9

"A man's mind stretched to a new idea never goes back to its original dimensions."

—*Oliver Wendell Holmes*

# Embrace Change and Innovation

Leapfrogging the competition requires change and innovation. It is not easy, but it is simple. While we don't have a choice about whether change happens, we do have a choice about how we react to it. The choice really boils down to this—either we manage change, or it will manage us.

In the long run, sameness is the fast track to mediocrity. And mediocre companies won't survive. Tuli Kupferberg said it best: "When patterns are broken, new worlds emerge." And that is your challenge—to convince your team that the new world you are trying to create is better than the one you're in. Is it easy? Of course not. It takes planning, commitment, patience, and courage.

But, also make sure that you focus on making the *right* changes, not just those that are easy. Take British Rail, for example. When the company had a real fall-off in business, they went looking for marketing answers and searched for a new ad agency, one that could deliver an ad campaign that would bring their customers back.

When the British Rail executives went to the offices of a prominent London ad agency to discuss their needs, they were met by a very rude receptionist who insisted they wait.

Finally, an unkempt person led them to a conference room— a dirty, scruffy room cluttered with plates of stale food. The executives were once again left to wait. A few agency people drifted in and out of the room, basically ignoring the executives who grew more impatient by the minute. When the execs tried to ask what was going on, the agency people brushed them off and went about their work.

Eventually, the executives had enough. As they angrily started to get up, completely disgusted with the way they'd been treated, an agency representative addressed them.

"Gentlemen," he said, "your treatment here at our agency is not typical of how we treat our clients—in fact, we've gone out of our way to stage this meeting for you. We've behaved this way to point out to you what it's like to be a customer of British Rail. Your real problem isn't your advertising; it's your people. We suggest you let us address your employee attitude problem before we attempt to change your advertising."

The British Rail executives were shocked, but the agency got the account! They had the remarkable conviction to point out the problem because it knew exactly what needed to change.

Change is not something to fear; it is a blessing. It is what makes life exciting. Great leaders not only know this—they embrace it. From a business management perspective, it is the very thing that fuels growth. Complacency and stagnation can crush even the greatest of companies. So can small, incremental improvements when the market is ripe for something radically different.

Take a good look at your market and industry. What one change or paradigm shift could send everyone else back to zero? What would really wow your customers? What latent need do they have that they might not even be aware of yet? Find out what their problems are and what their customers' problems are. What would make their lives easier? Examine every interaction with them. How do you communicate with them? How do they communicate with you? How do you invoice them? How do you fill orders with them? How do you train people, including your customers? What alternatives exist? Are you using video training? Think YouTube. Are you using interactive, real-time communication and feedback? Are you going paperless? Are you exploring Vendor-Managed Inventory Control (VMIC) with your suppliers, where you no longer order from them, but they stock you in standardized, controlled ways? Where is the non-value-added activity in your business, and what are you doing to eliminate it? Where are you at risk? What are your competitors doing better than you? Do you know?

Today, it is often riskier to sit still in business than it is to act. Teach your team to look for and appreciate change. Teach them to connect dots that seem unrelated. Keep in mind that many of the greatest discoveries and innovations came from original mistakes or failures.

The truth, of course, is that change can be a wonderful gift. In fact, it is the key that unlocks the doors to growth and excitement in any organization. And, most importantly, without it, your competition will pass you by. A big part of success, as a leader, will be your ability to inspire your team to get out of their comfort zones, to assure them that even though they are on a new path, it's the right path, for the right reasons.

# CHECKLIST FOR SUCCESS

✓ Leapfrogging the competition requires change and innovation.

✓ Embrace and inspire change by leading with passion, courage, and spirit.

✓ Suspend judgment, and allow your mind to stretch and imagine a variety of alternatives.

✓ Know that there is more than one way to solve a problem.

✓ Actively look for the one thing that could be game-changing.

✓ Challenge your assumptions and paradigms, and teach others to do the same.

✓ Explore multiple options before making a choice.

"I don't know where we should take this company, but I do know that if I start with the right people, ask them the right questions, and engage them in vigorous debate, we will find a way to make this company great."

— *James Collins*

# About the
# Authors

# MAC ANDERSON

Mac Anderson is the founder of Simple Truths and Successories, Inc., the leader in designing and marketing products for motivation and recognition. However, these companies are not the first success stories for Mac. He was also the founder and CEO of McCord Travel, the largest travel company in the Midwest, and part owner and vice president of sales and marketing for the Orval Kent Company, the country's largest manufacturer of prepared salads.

His accomplishments in these unrelated industries provide some insight into his passion and leadership skills. He also brings the same passion to speaking to many corporate audiences on a variety of topics, including leadership, motivation, and team building.

Mac has authored or coauthored twenty-six books that have sold more than four million copies. Some of his titles include:

*212°: The Extra Degree*

*212° Service: The 10 Rules for Creating a Service Culture*

*Best of Success: A Treasury of Inspiration*

*Change Is Good… You Go First: 21 Ways to Inspire Change*

*Charging the Human Battery: 50 Ways to Motivate Yourself*

*Customer Love: Great Stories about Great Service*

*The Essence of Leadership*

*Habits Die Hard: 10 Steps to Building Successful Habits*

*The Nature of Success*

*The Power of Attitude*

*The Power of Kindness*

*Things That Grab Your Heart and Won't Let Go:*
    *Stories That Will Give You Goose Bumps*

*To a Child, Love Is Spelled T-I-M-E: What a Child Really*
    *Needs from You*

*What's the Big Idea?: How One Idea Can Change Your*
    *Business and Your Life*

*You Can't Send a Duck to Eagle School: And Other*
    *Simple Truths of Leadership*

# JOHN J. MURPHY

John J. Murphy is an award-winning author, speaker, and management consultant. Drawing on a diverse collection of team experiences as a corporate manager, consultant, and collegiate quarterback, John has appeared on more than five hundred radio and television stations, and his work has been featured in more than fifty newspapers nationwide.

As founder and president of Venture Management Consultants (www.venturemanagementconsultants .com), John specializes in creating high-performance team environments, teaching leadership and team development, and leading global kaizen events. He has trained thousands of change agents from more than fifty countries and has helped some of the world's leading organizations design and implement positive change.

John is a critically acclaimed author and sought-after speaker. His books include:

*Pulling Together: 10 Rules for High Performance Teams*

*Zentrepreneur: Get Out of the Way and Lead, Create a Culture of Innovation and Fearlessness*

*Beyond Doubt: Four Steps to Inner Peace*

*Reinvent Yourself: A Lesson in Personal Leadership*

*Agent of Change: Leading a Cultural Revolution*

*Sage Leadership: Awakening the Spirit in Work*

*Get a Real Life: A Lesson in Personal Empowerment*

*The Eight Disciplines: An Enticing Look into Your Personality*

*Habits Die Hard: 10 Steps to Building Successful Habits*

*Leading with Passion: 10 Essentials for Inspiring Others*

*The How of Wow: Secrets to World Class Service*

*Half-Full: Your Perception Becomes Your Reality*

# TAKE THE LEAP.
## GET OUT IN FRONT.

The view is terrific,
and there's a lot less traffic.